SHEER POETRY

Roger Elkin

Sheer Poetry

© Roger Elkin

First Edition 2020
ISBN: 978-1-913329-16-7

Roger Elkin has asserted his authorship and given his permission to Dempsey & Windle for these poems to be published here.

All rights reserved. No part of this publication may be reproduced, stored in a retrieval system or transmitted in any form or by any means without the written consent of the author, nor otherwise circulated in any form of binding or cover other than that in which it is published and without a similar condition being imposed on a subsequent purchaser.

Published by Dempsey & Windle
15 Rosetrees
Guildford
Surrey
GU1 2HS
UK
01483 571164
dempseyandwindle.com

British Library Cataloguing-in-Publication Data

A catalogue record for this book is available from the British Library.

For Eileen,
> who, like me, understands
> that there's more to being
> well-versed as a climber
> than knowing the ropes ...

Acknowledgements
are due to the editors of the various magazines and anthologies in which versions of these poems first appeared:

Agenda; *Bridgewater & Other Poems*; *Envoi*; *Hungry Hill Writing*; *Into the Void Anthology*; *Luminous Echoes*; *Milestones, the Anthology* 2017; *Poets Meet Politics Anthology* 2015; *Prole*; *Salpeot; Segora Festival Edition* 2010-2012; *Sentinel Poetry Quarterly*; *Sharp as Lemons*; *The Fenland Read*; *The Ver Prize 2016 Anthology*; *The Yeovil Literary Prize* 2012-2013; *Ware Poets 15th Competition Anthology 2013*; *We Will Be Free, The Bread and Roses Poetry Award Anthology 2018*; *Wells Festival of Literature 25th Anniversary Anthology; Welsh Poetry Competition* Anthology 2012-2016; *Wolverhampton Literature Festival Poetry* Anthology 2018; *Wow! Words on the Waves Anthology* 2015.

The following poems have been awarded prizes in (inter)national Open Poetry Competitions:

Gran's Living-Room Triptych	1st	**Southport Writers' Circle**	2015
Icarus considers his Dad's feather-fixation	2nd	**Penfro**	2017
Mapping the Past	3rd	**Barnet**	2012
North Ferriby Foreshore, remembering	1st	**Segora**	2012
Poor-man's Racehorse	3rd	**Philip Larkin Society**	2014
Saving face with Grandpa	1st	**Link Age, Southwark**	2018
Soldiering	2nd	**Buzzwords**	2018
Songs Without Words	1st	**Buxton**	2016
Task Force	1st	**Sentinel Quarterly**	2012
The Longest Day	1st	**Poetry on the Lake (Cinema)**	2018

CONTENTS

Being two-faced	9
Surfeits of love: the silences	10
The sudden end of the man who kept his garden tidy	12
Of clints and grykes	13
Sheer Poetry: Considering the Egyptian Position	14
Of Love & Sex, & the Problem of Gendering	15
Trawling photos of David Bowie sporting eye-liner	16
Pencil drawing of a girl, circa 1912, partially erased	17
Living for Art, Living for Love: Auntie Reenie sings *Vissi d'arte* from **Tosca**	18
Songs Without Words	20
Standing at the Pleyel grand-piano	22
The Good Thing About My Chiropracticer	24
Eddie's Mozart Bequest	26
Lang Lang Plays Mozart's *Piano Sonata in B flat major*, *K333*	28
Icarus considers his Dad's feather-fixation	30
Dreaming of Flying	32
Leda: Her Memory of Feathers	34
Sharing our son's out of darkness moment	35
Obsession Confession	36
Mapping the Past	37
the brother he never really knew	38
For the life of them	40
Handing On: Look After This Baby	42
Graham, our neighbour	43

Ireland's Blight
I: *Ireland's 9/11*   44
II: *Cooking Cabbages*   46
III: *Beggars' Meal – "Indian Buck"*   48
IV: *Task Work*   49
V: *Summing Up*   51

The Politics of Class
I: *Poor-man's racehorse*   53
II: *Class Act*   54
III: *Classy Statues*   54

The Black & White Divisions   56
Moving On: Jo, the Crossing Sweeper from **Bleak House**   58
Fishing the Khabur River, Syria   60
This is the village   62
Gran's Living-Room Triptych   64
Saving face with Grandpa and not being huffed   66
Soldiering   68
North Ferriby Foreshore, remembering   70
Being Waspish   72
The Longest Day   73
Of the spaces between   74
Patchwork Language   76
Shoplifting   78

Being two-faced

The Latin for door, *ianua*, lends January
our opening on the year:
that start of things that is the end of things.

Coming or going it's the same wintry litany:

    Celtish   dark month, dead month
    Saxon   *wulfmanoth* (weather so raw, wolves preyed on folk)
    Finnish   *tammikuu* (the winter's heart)
    Czech   *leden* (iced month)
    Ukrainian month of cutting wind
    Croatian   month of slicing wind
    Belarusian the frosty one.

Only   Turkish   *ocak* (stove, hearth)
centres it anywhere near home.

But here, in London, this January it's been -4 degrees
and on Oxford Street, going or coming, going and coming,
shop doors have been open wide:

the wasted heat   wasted energy   the waste.

But doesn't end there.
Surely you can't have forgotten the old folk-rhyme:

> *Summer in winter and a summer's flood*
> *Never boded England good.*

It is more than Janus that is two-faced.

Out in the Pacific, atolls are drowning.

Surfeits of love: the silences

What troubles her most are the silences
coming as they do when he's growling away again
in counterpoint rehearsing the familiar themes
fortissimo　　　　　*sforzandi*　　　*crescendo*
but with even more variations this time round
and all she can think of doing to save the piece
is close down her ears
and count the beats
count them　　　count them

It's those silences – long, held,
longer held – cutting against the rhythm
that make it hard to know when/whether/where
she can pick up the tune again
so has lost herself
in her own karaoke-show
with the volume turned to zero
and hamming the role so well
she's kidded him into thinking
she's still singing the old clichés
from the same old hymn sheet

He hasn't seen her
mouthing the words and leafing through
the empty score of herself
hasn't heard this new song she's tumbled into
where　　　　going solo　　　she's convincing herself
there'll be no more silences

No   no more silences
just rests   rests
yes, she'll leave him
plenty of rests

He'll count them
how he'll count them

The sudden end of the man who kept his garden tidy

Scissors, black-handled and hanging
on a tack hammered at the back
of his garage, smack against the jamb
of what the sales spec for this "executive
house" framed "the personnel door".
Watched them tick-tocking as he jostled
them in passing, though they never
clattered off – just swung mid-air,
threatening activity.

How his face waxed in satisfaction
with that broad smile and fanatical
wide-eyed stare when he reached them
free to whetstone, wipe and shine
the menace of their wide-open blades,
then tested their bevelled edge against
his sliding finger – oh, so skilled he never
spilled his blood.

Only know this since his sister, face
swollen and bruised, tells me she's left him.
And how, each summer dusk, lifting them
down he prowled around their back-garden,
flash-light in his left hand, scissors
snip-snipping in his right. *Hundreds*,
he numbered. *Hundreds this month,*
as he slugged away his sliding enemy.

She tells me how till today
she'd writhed silently inside to counterpoint
their silent writhing. His sudden end,
her Eden compromised: the scissors
in his back.

Of clints and grykes

I   Sounding like body parts, and womanly-vulnerable
at that, there's no doubt it was blokes who named them.
Yes, more "dirty words" for our lads to pass around

         with Dad's filched cigs behind the school bike sheds.
How those fifth formers sniggered. They'd clocked
the monosyllables all right - northern and brunt -

         but not cottoned on to the extra letters.
The reason? Minds obsexed from youth.
(Is it any wonder that men can't multitask ...

II   Decades later, standing above Malham Cove,
I can't help but notice the limestone pavement,
how its surface gleams like spread limbs

         offered for massage, and held so still:
the fissures' given dimples, the alabaster shading,
the patina of pampering and age.

III   Back home, trying to identify plant specimens
from this kingdom of clints and grykes, I'm sure
the men have been sexing things up again:

         what with ferns named rigid buckler, and hart's-tongue.
And there's biting stonecrop, prickly sedge, hairy rock-cress;
plus enchanter's nightshade, and bloody crane'sbill;

         not to mention lady's bedstraw, and wild thyme -
all topped by maidenhair. Oh, that maidenhair.
Where would men be without that maidenhair ...

Sheer Poetry: Considering the Egyptian Position

Ever thought that lying spreadeagled as if trying
to get deep inside the body of rock is the nearest
you'll come to making love in public? And yet
it's so intimate this tryst that can't be missed

right from that instance when at a distance
you catch a first glimpse, and your gut flutters
then slowly worms to churning as you draw near
and you know you've just got to get on top.

What attracts is the straddling reach although
the surface is cold - even hostile - as though it doesn't
want to know you, and you're wanting to own it all
if only for the moment, not let go. How your fingers

crimp and gingerly inch in each fissure and crack.
And how it warms to the body-heat of your touch
with the air between you like shared breathing,
as you feel your heartbeats echoing iambically

beneath you. No foetal position this, secure
and comfortably womb-cocooned, but named
The Egyptian after the bent knee and toehold
etched in death celebrations on a temple wall.

What if you should fall? Sheer poetry. Shakespeare
knew all about that: arrival as death. And rest assured
even if there's no abseil available, you will be
brought breathlessly back down to earth again.

Of Love & Sex, & the Problem of Gendering

They've got it wrong, the Germans, naming
the beach as masculine - *der Strand* – when,
just strolling along Formby foreshore, shows
it's clearly female, wide-eyed and going deeper
than surfaces. They're daft, too, neutering

James Joyce's "scrotum-tightening" sea into
a sexless *das Meer*. For one, it's all woman,
with her cockteaser attractiveness under rain
as getting testily-petulant she turns down sand;
and, two, when the tide's full out, and its etched

horizon is miles away, (whether it's scorching
sun or louring cloud that threatens) she makes it
worth your trekking there to taste her allure.
Once back on shore again, they're partly right
with dunes – *die Dünen* - their shifting plurality

like recumbent sculptures of lossocking women
their limbs trickle-lifting, rising and falling
as if disturbed mid-dream, then resettling,
while keeping close to chest those ruttings and
rootings of natterjack toads and marram grass.

And can't complain about what they've done to
sand - *die Sand* - as it slips womanly-vulnerable
through fingers, like love - *die Liebe.* But then,
being English - masculine, feminine, whatever –
love is love: just that - the sex already understood ...

Trawling photos of David Bowie sporting eye-liner

and it's neighbour Smith fresh from finishing his shift
at Florence Colliery as, snap-tin in hand, he crosses
the cobbled yard, and clacking the back door latch,
looms four-square in the scullery gloom, his doe-eyes
almond-shaped by coal dust.

And I'm picturing him, stripped to singlet,
standing at the slopstone and getting stuck into shaving,
his cut-throat rasping skin and sashaying around chin.
What a show - so quickly skilful, little finger delicately
extended. And never a nick. Once done, turns
as he always turns for approval, his cheeks shiny-red.
And redder against his lashes' coal dust mascara.

But it is his eye-smiles mapped in the shaving-glass
that conspire an admission of sorts. For sure,
knows nothing about AC/DC – except electrics.
Knows only where he's going. And that's where
he's been since barely a man, like his Dad, and
his Dad's Dad before him. Deep beneath, hacking at
back-breaking graft, the coal shards indigoing to black
splintering under his skin. The dust clogging hair-line,
and eye-lining eyes in an innocence that commands
no mannered photo-posed rehearsal: but AC/DC smiles
working deep for him, underground.

Pencil drawing of a girl, circa 1912, partially erased

"The beauty of the seemingly insignificant" Noel Connor

Who knows its significance,
the hidden beauty of this pencil sketch
that catches the glimmer of a likeness -

the cross-hatching, blocking-in
and shading of her eyes, those
lips, that hair - but didn't quite

satisfy, so has been rubbed out
to smudged Summer clouds
dulling the sky's blank page.

Rather than the captured
factualities, it is the erasure's
what-might-have-beens

that admit appearances.
But then, how readily
we grow dispirited; give up;

so try to erase what others
might deem our failures.
And how we mythologize

in recreating the past. Hers. Ours.
How we draw to cover the tracks.
And rub. Rub.

Living for Art, Living for Love
Auntie Reenie sings *Vissi d'arte* from *Tosca*

Classix Nite and at the Club's upright piano
sits Bob Pierce, tall and swarthy with more than
a touch of the negro in him, that's why he can do
that gravelly Satchmo take-off folk regularly demand …

but tonight he's accompanying Reenie's spot –
her standing, hands clasped, operatic,
crimsoned lips pursed and primped, hair perm-rinsed,
waved, curled, crimped, and eyes glinting …
her stance that half-angled shoulder pose
she's seen at the *Theatre Royal*, head erect,
breath kept ready, then once Bob has insinuated
the intro, goes glowingly into song …

> *I lived for art, I lived for love*

her voice
pouring sweetly, ringing like fine wine
and laddering the staves, a sort of
honeyed spun thread treading the scales

> *I sent up my song to the stars,*
> *to the skies*

not a warbling, but pure and fulsome,
though despite her heaving chest, her mouth's
bright flowering, not quite making it, the top notes
sliding and cracking

> *Why oh Lord,*
> *why do you reward me thus*

and your Mum's shoulders lifting
in cringing embarrassment (though staying
dumb) while sister Flo hisses *Christ*!

and, as the applause water-falls, Reenie's
breathing freely again, nodding Bob acknowledgment
till flashes a glance at husband Les that sends him
scarpering off, glass of Bass in hand,
to fetch her her second Cherry B,
all the while the barstaff humming

why do you reward me thus

Songs Without Words

What really stuck in Mum's craw that next Summer
was surrendering her Bechstein baby grand,
that altar of arrival at which she'd taken daily stock
of her upbringing, and her mother's sacrifice
putting her to the upright. Oh, how she'd ladedahed
at family and friends as graduating to this black-lacquered
anvil straddling the corner of her living room.

So would tackle it, side-saddling the piano-stool's moquette,
hands lifting and flashing, trafficking the ruffles of notes
as if the caressing of ivories, the spread-fingered rending
were her sole hope of regaining self.

There she'd put all her stumbling discord
back together again with the sweet-saccharine
middle-class fanciness of those *Songs Without Words*,
the genius of Mendelssohn - uncircumcised Jewboy
become good Lutheran - in sister Fanny's filigree piano-pieces:
musical antimaccassars covering the vulnerabilities
of nothingness, the notes clustering
like sticky flies sucking at ripe blackberries
while Dad smiled wryly with his put-on face,
his fingers itching to switch his TV back to life.

So, from the moment the piano left -
        legs rag-swagged for protection,
        then jacked into the back
        of Cheetham's van —
she felt abandoned.

All that time, she kept schtum,
silently rehearsing
her versions of words without songs.

Standing at the Pleyel grand-piano,

Chopin, momentarily released
from the keyboard's regimentals, its blacks, its whites,
glances through the casement window
down to the Nohant gardens below
where in the early June morning, a-fizz with insects
and that special celebratory mid-France light,
he sees Sands – his *Aurore* to her *Chip-Chip* – trawling the lawns,
a swathe of late lilac and early roses flowing over her arms

and pictures her arranging them at her salon's wild-cherry table,
her pollen-spent complexion deeping into dark braided hair
and bundled at her ears. Her chastised-spaniel eyes, velvet rich.
Her thin lips. The interrogation of her nose.

Sees her in her man-clothes –
       jacket, trousers, waistcoat, cravat,
       the worn-at-heel shoes -
sees the peek of white flesh at the nape of her neck,
her jaunty back, her broad hips
as facing away she places
the lilac, the scent-heavy roses
their mouths agape – leaning, leaning -
and he knows it is not earth on her fingers,
but tree-moss and twig smirch.
He knows this is not love.

So turns to the mazurka he's working
in perfection of its remembered territory,
this distant picture of Poland
> the languorous rubato,
> the heart-aching fall from major to minor,
> its plangent harmonies,
> the tender swaying wave-racing rhythms,
> its harsh sonorities and sinister dissonances
> > windmilling then collapsing,
> its stolen tempo folding away

and knows this is earth.
This is love.
This magic worth living the present for.

The Good Thing About My Chiropracticer

Not the carefully careless ease with which
she swears at everything. *Take it or bloody
leave it, the treatment's what you're bleeding
well here for, so strip down to your pants.*

Not her ex-forces side-kick, Mick, who keeps
the books in pencil and regales waiting patients
with home-spun cures for upset guts, then sidles
upstairs to play with his gaming station.

Not Dandy her plug-ugly rust-coloured dog
Mummy's bleeding lovely beast who gets randy
with your leg, pants steam-train-madly to be let out,
and slashes up the passage when he isn't.

Not the way she nubs and pummels your spine,
zags your legs crossing over, tugs arm, then cricks
your neck, again, again, saying *You're getting
bloody better* as you're wincing in agreement.

Not the hard-luck stories of restoring
her retirement pad in France which punctuate
her laying on of hands, all the time confirming
You really need to come twice a bleeding week.

None of this: but the fact that the ice-pack
sessions on small of back and nape of neck
recommended three times daily for thirty minutes
lying flat, knees bent at forty-five degrees

and listening to CDs are just long enough
to let you resolve the problem of bringing things
to resolution in Mozart's piano concertos –
oh, so anti-inflammatory.

No wonder things are getting so much
bleeding better with each rippling of notes.

Eddie's Mozart Bequest

For My friend, if and when he'd penned in ink
on the pink post-it sellotaped inside
the frontispiece. Surely he didn't think

by that *if* he'd survive while others died?
After all, he'd been near to death before:
as a child coughing up gobbings of blood

like flowers; and later, soldiering, he saw
several squaddies serving alongside him
dis-limbed and killed in furnaces of war:

Lucky escape, he'd quipped. *Wasn't my time
just then – still to come*, though knew not *never*
despite hiding behind that *if* – a form

of lying. It was the *when* he'd mither
about all day, then long into the night
once he'd stopped work, werriting on whether

he'd be hospitalized, or perhaps might
drop off the perch while driving, *hurt other
folk,* or fade away, alone, out of sight.

So, to save his wife unneeded bother
at his death, he'd signed this facsimile
cataloguing Mozart's output over

to me. Inside the book's wallpapery
sleeve, page following page of neat ruled staves
record the music's tread in spidery

notes. Good to see that though Mozart contrives
to tie invention down by penning list
in tempi, bars, key signatures, octaves

there's no *if and when* for him. Optimist,
he'd planned his notebook to reach far in time
for, balancing what he's scored, there's almost

as many empty pages: *Death defined
by absences.* I'm thrilled to get this book -
Eddie's bequest – better by far than mine:

these words. But suspect Eddie might not like
such notes; want silences to chart his wake.

In 1990, the British Museum printed *Mozart's Thematic Catalogue*, a copy of the hand-written list where Mozart charted the opening bars of his works as he wrote them, from 1784 till three weeks before his death in 1791.

Lang Lang Plays Mozart's *Piano Sonata in B flat major, K333*

With his face …

>acting it all out like a fresh fairy-tale he's just
>stumbled into, its twists and turns mirrored
>in his mimed surprise: nose sniffing keys,
>or twitching at runs; mouth smiling at music's
>slide to harmony; brow frowning in feigned pain
>as the bass grows heavy; lips lowering in ambush
>of trills; or beaming with relief at expected modulation,
>the notes negotiating towards resolution …

With his eyes …

>pupils jigging, sliding, and smiling.
>Rolls them. Lets drop. Lifts. And glazes over
>as gazing above and beyond. Head rocking
>forward. And back. Face sliding side to side.
>Eyes skittering as the music trips into arpeggio
>and scale … and steadying again. Lights of eyes
>lighting up in delight, his clarity of vision picking
>out the notes' division in their own black and white …

With his hands ...

> plunging in, and down, having fun
> with his searching fingers, as if the piano is baby
> or impish kitten flat out on its back. Tickles its belly.
> Then retracts each hand in turn, lashing back
> in flashing arc, almost as though his wrists are elastic.
> And descends to teasing again, rippling
> the living rhythm, digging music's innerness
> till mastered within his slipping fingertips ...

With face, eyes, hands

> Lang Lang plays Mozart off by heart ...

Icarus considers his Dad's feather-fixation

For weeks he's roamed the lanes and fields stopping
to glean feathers, no matter their colour
or formation. His aim is a grouping

of range in size and shape, their curvature
so precisely-fanned that he has devised
the wings' full-spanned arc. It seemed so bizarre

at first: the flimsy down, the bigger-sized
plumes, the pinion quills: all so disparate
and slight. Yet from such fluff he's organized

the means to create our release from Crete
where king Minos, blocking off our escape
by land and sea, forced Dad to contemplate

using *"Apollo's gifts"* to summon up
his plans. Such wealth of covert, filoplume,
retrices, and contour feathers that shape

the wing! What artistry as handling them
he fondles barbules, smooths them flat, unfluffs
their tips to blading edge, and starts to comb

them straight! But placing them's the taxing stuff.
The frame is elm – *Used*, he claims, *because its
whittled limbs have "give". Doesn't work when stiff.*

And we can't put any old feather just
where we like – *Have to match the marked-out scheme
and grading chart*; and, you've guessed, he'll insist

on fixing them. First, with wax plundered from
wild bees (but taking care he'll not get stung).
He'll stick the quills with this. Then, to confirm

all's safe, he'll tie the plumes midpoint with string.
That way, Dad says, *we'll both soon be swooping
free. No chance under the sun our going wrong ...*

Dreaming of Flying

"The moment you doubt whether you can fly, you cease for ever to be able to do it"
J. M. Barrie, **Peter Pan**

She's always wanted to fly
that's why she's brought those grown-up wings
she usually hangs – widespread, pinned –
in her bedroom – a dangling, hanging reminder
she's always wanted to fly

She's always wanted to fly
not like angels in some da Vinci painting,
holily po-faced with silver glistening wings
but something closer to earth, with just a wincey-bit
of fantasy, hence these three-feet-six
Disney-things of wings
she's always wanted to fly

She's always wanted to fly
that's why she drop-lipped and tantrummed,
even squeezed a wet-eyed cry, pestering Mum
till she got these shop-made wings
framed from veiling, so that, flouncy-skirt bouncy,
she could fly away - big purple fairy-butterfly
she's always wanted to fly

She's always wanted to fly
and rising higher, *higher*, HIGH
break her face into smiling
while watching her masks
fall, layer after layer, spiralling
nightmarishly away
she's always wanted to fly

wanted to fly
to fly
fly

wonder why

Leda: Her Memory of Feathers

Right from the start what niggled me
was all that down.

I could handle the scapulars and hackles,
could accept their sunshiny brightness;
and even when they weren't fully-formed
but a smudged beigy-grey
just about manage the coverts.
No, it was those fiddling filaments,
that fluffing unpindownable stuff,
which threw me.

That, and the yellow neb, crocus-gold against white
with its nibbling ridge – indigo to Prussian blue –
like the scribble of larches at the edge
of a windswept snowscape, bare-spaced
and smelling of separateness.
Not to mention the snorting taunts,
that hiss, insisting.
And his eyes. Those peevish eyes.

All that alarmed. But not half as much
as his weight. The blood-pulse. His heart-beat.
And the purposeful lift of limbs, trembling
to begin with, then wrapping angrily,
the air displaced.

Such a long neck. Snaking between breasts.
The weight of him. Those waxy black talons.
His pinioned wing feathers folding around me,
holding me close.
Those feathers, their ungentle presence.
The everywhereness of down.

Sharing our son's out of darkness moment

So, this is the lad whose first word
was *Moon, Moon* his face pleating
in recognition and seeking applause,
though, no doubt at forty-plus, he
won't recall all this, he's so enthralled
with his latest craze - a telescope.

We're here, mid-France, in the middle
of the countryside, fields harvest-gleaned
for miles, and cicadas tzinging beneath
a night sky bigger/wider than imagining,
and blacker than black: a vast caul of indigo
that's wrapped up daylight and fashioned
its package with stars. And there, hugging
the horizon, the moon. Huge. Smiling.

Before we know it, we're squatting on the floor,
our knees and elbows spraunged, and hands
and eyes vying for focus as trying to place
the moon squarely, bring into view the craters
that make its face, and scan its pale lemon disc
etched out of darkness.

He's all beaming face in possession now
of a new world of words - *ocular, refraction,
resolution, aperture, magnification* ...

Such big differences crossed,
this getting near. And how illuminating,
the shared scope in the monosyllables
of mum, dad, son.
Of moon. Of love.

Obsession Confession

It's the way she holds her head slightly askew
and smiles that full beam revealing her teeth
and slick of lips, her brown eyes lighting up,
her brow dipping, ears leaning, head nodding
then bending forward and back again, taking
a deep breath almost as though this is the last
thing she'll have chance to do, this very moment
the one she'll remember when she's on her own,
locked into her own world, own loneliness when
he's finally gone all that way away and she hasn't
any hope of getting to see him, sort of dropping in
casually as she would if he lived just around
the corner, but she's conscious that she's frowning
now and has to make that effort to put that smile
back in its place, dig deep to remake her beaming
face, her body almost pouring out of her skin as if
she's trying to hold him, smother him, bring him
close to her, wanting to get inside him, never let him
go away because she knows they'll be all right though
he's miles away from her so has to check her tears,
pick up her smiles, make sure he's sure it's him
she's smiling for, him she's missing, only him,
her deaf and dumb grandson

Mapping the Past

Remember, she said, *we'll have time enough*.
But you need more than a walk, and/or map
to rediscover yourself. For sure, I recall the path,
arrow-straight along the cliff-edge flanking
the windswept ash, the open-common land
where nesting blackbirds crackerjacked at our
tramping approach, both startled and startling.

And, yes, the gravel chippings chuntered underfoot
the same, as we dropped down the flight of steps
with their shuttered boards zig-zagging between
gorse and bramble. Surely here the pathway turned
to offer a vista as wide open as childhood: the sea
shading from light to grey as the sunshine clouded
over. Drawing near the pebbled shore, we could hear
the gulls screaling as they picked over bladderwrack
blistering at the tide's edge with its flotsam offerings.

Here we ran, hand in hand, as children. Made friends.
Lost innocence. Was where we grew aware of our
parents, their differences, as listening through the dark
we heard their whispers turning into shouts, till drowned
by the turnings of the sea, its tumbling uncertainties ...

Remember she said, *We'll have time enough*. But,
once lost, is lost. And never, the right time to recover.

the brother he never really knew

passed himself off from whenever as *bigger where it
matters* and because it was the one ace he held in his hand
let it go to his head becoming Dad's *Big-I-am That's him*

asthmatic too but didn't stop him dipping fingers into Mum's
handbag so that ever after it sat at her side or else she'd cry
Bag Me bag Where's me bag nor stop him unpicking the lock

of Dad's coming-of-age desk to nick riffled quids elastic-banded
just a couple at a time for fags smoked since was six so never
caught up with his twin sister but bragged his big-headed time

bad-ladding it around our town and had the crap leather-belted out
of him, belted back in Dad strapping his backside *You nowt You
nowt* till twigged he could run quicker so legged it upstairs slipped

through window streamed across lean-to roof and spraunged over
back-garden wall running towards flunking the 11+ to sec-mod
with mates Ben-Gunning his pimply adolescence through school play

the nearest he'd come to his **Treasure Island** fagging ten a day
behind bike-sheds his tapered nails nicotined and passing-out
big-dicked himself to hashish ransacking Chemists for acid tabs

sent down and again after petty-cashing stamps and flashed back
again and again longer spell this time around for shipping grass
from Spain inside back tyres of hired white van Dad railing

Micky Spillane Clink's too good for him but once freed reformed
in sorts played weekly drumming-gigs with Hutch's Band in clubs
and pubs got the beat from beating his meat among other things

Mum always said *Should have been a butcher* till that Christmas Eve
back from festive jamming session sat with first can of the night
in right hand fag-tab in the left was found next morning *Whata*

Chrissy pressie by Sam the down-and-outer he'd roomed to shelter
from everything he'd been through found whammed out of life
just fifty-seven heart bust apart and I only know cos Sam contacted

that *effing git of a brother* he never really knew

For the life of them

The Adidas logo from his sneaker soles
zig-zagging across the village green
betrayed the way he'd taken
kicking into touch their Home Sweet Home
with its *Pleases* and *Thankyous*,
its *Don't speak till you're spoken to*,
its *Elbows off the table, lad.*

Snatch-grabbing his black hoody,
he'd tantrummed - *I'm bloodywell going* –
banging the back door, latch clacking,
the whole house shaking.
Dad stone-stiff. *Language, lad.*
Mam a trapped animal, her heart
torn apart, crying, *And don't even think
of coming back till you're sorry.*

Two days later, ransacking their minds,
they listed what he'd been wearing:
> the red T-shirt
> that hoody
> his new Denim slimfits – *Them's his best*
> the with-it odd socks – *How daft is that*
> those sneakers.

Couldn't for the life of them
begin to think why/where he'd gone.
Questioned his friends.
Triple-checked for messages.

Waited.

Waited for a phone call.
The backdoor latch rattling.
The shuffle up the creaking stairs.

They waited,
guilt riddling their thinking,
stalking their mornings,
haunting their sleep.

Three months later, the mere reeds
parted in passing:
the water a sudden flush of red.
And there, a sneaker adrift ...

Handing On: Look After This Baby

You will not remember this: your legs
delicately held at ankle like a trussed-up chicken
ready for pulling; bum suspended, the rest of you
grounded, helpless, yet all-chuckling eye-smiles
in that inbuilt trust at my ease, a sort of comfortable
smugness that, for sure, will make you forget
the indignity of it.

As for those swipes of the cottonwool pad –
not too cold, not too wet – as they wipe down
the new-old skin, its wrinkles and folds,
then talcing and drying round the crease
before creaming, cool and soothing –
believe me, you'll retain not a jot of this.

And yet decades later it will all come
tumbling back – uneasily, perhaps, at first,
perhaps even painful facing the old-new skin,
the fumbling touch, the panic flash of eyes,
the grounded helplessness. But in time you'll
become a dab hand at it as giving bedbaths to
your unchuckling Mum thankful for handing this on.

Graham, our neighbour,

(aka *"The Major"*) surveys his half-acre kingdom
daily, inspecting the gravel and Cuprinol salients
that keep insurgencies at bay – though doesn't stand
a chance in the Spring Offensive against the snails

he lobs sailing over fences – not to mention
that entrenched enemy, the yellow loosestrife.
Says *The name's enough to give the game away*,
as he slashes at it, then piles it high in pyres,

and, when it lances back, grows stiff redoubling
the attack. How he thrills at the spilled innernesses
of those red lily-beetles screaling beneath his heels.
Says blood's his favourite colour *Commands respect.*

But then it's always been more than a private's war.
That's why he decorates the pride of his wife
with the knifing stripes of her ordered lawns,
and treats his kids like weeds, dishing out jankers

For the good of it. Gets high on their fazed-away gaze.
He's a born stonewaller: so gives no ground away.
And never stands at ease. Just marks time. Marks time.
With death his lieutenant only has life to fear.

Ireland's Blight

I: Ireland's 9/11

After the sacking of Drogheda

> when the garrison, having been asked,
> according to military etiquette, three times to surrender
> and, refusing,
> its walls were stormed;
> the governor, Sir Arthur Aston, battered to death;
> and his three thousand garrison defenders,
> along with hundreds of civilians, put to the sword,
> the Model Army defending themselves
> by using children as bucklers;
>
> and when, some hours later, several citizens
> seeking refuge in St. Peter's steeple
> where refusing to "yield to mercy",
> the doors were barricaded against their coming out
> and pews smashed to pieces for fire-wood
> these trapped Catholics were burnt, screaming, alive
> with their children,

The Lord Protector of Ireland asserted

> *This was a righteous judgement of God*
> *upon those barbarous wretches*

for, as the Psalmist writes

> *Happy shall he be that taketh and dasheth*
> *thy children against the stones.* *

Or, put more succinctly,

> *Nits make lice.*

---

*Oliver Cromwell, justifying the massacre of children at the sacking of Drogheda, September 11th 1649

II: Cooking Cabbages

Delia's How To Cook, Book Two, (1999), p121

Naming them an *Absolute work of art*
and claiming *One medium-sized cabbage will serve four*
Delia confesses she's questioned for decades
how best to cook them:

whether it's the Round Cabbage …

> (Impossible unwrapping its packed bandages
> to release one complete leaf squeaking
> as it unpeels, layer after layer, till surrendering
> its heart, bone-white and smooth. Tapped, it sounds
> hollow. Hard. Like a child's skull.)

or the pointed Spring …

> (Young greens of thing. Discard those stripped-off
> floppy outers that hang, tired, like flapping skin
> of folks with malnutrition. Splice out their rib-thin
> stalks, white like clacking bones.
> Hear its heart squeal as it's ripped apart.)

the plusher, fuller Savoy …

> (Its skin the furred skin of scurvy, rough and coarse
> as scabby sores; or acid-green like slimed tripes
> before bleaching, its meshy texture of dressed seam,
> or honeycomb. Read it like Braille. Slowly.
> It's a scrotal sack in the dark. Cut it. Feel it squeal.)

or the fatter January King ...

       (Bird's-eye of patchwork grass, veined by
       dry-stone lime-walls; or crepe of collapsed
       lungs under famine autopsy; skin leather-crinkled,
       and leaf-tips tinged with purpura as if bruised.
       Stroked, it's known to squeal. Sliced, it cries.)

Faced with large-scale hunger
would Delia be half so poetical,
or, cutting words, be satisfied
with squeaks, cries and squeals...

In the Strokestown region during the Great Irish Famine "7,500 people were existing on boiled cabbage leaves once in forty-eight hours."
Roscommon Constabulary Report, October 12th 1846

III: Beggars' Meal - "Indian buck"

"The country is abundantly supplied with wheat and oats, the prices are most encouraging for sale, but nevertheless for payment of rent they are exported to Liverpool and Scotland, and the people, deprived of this resource, call out on the government for Indian corn, which requires time for its importation."
Sir Randolph Routh to Trevelyan,
Commissariat Correspondence, i, page 104

In France, they batten ganders down
with some paraphernalia of metal and leather,
so strapping each goose – solid, whole, still –
legs straddled, and feet trapped yet gangling mid-
air, the snake-head held high, beak forced gaping-up
with slicked tongue licking out, in, out –
orange against black – its gizzard visible
in the stretched neck's full length,
eyes swivelling in distress – and, there,
the basin-cum-tundish, regularly kept filled
with sun-bright corn-grits as brittle and glistening
as grave-chippings, in perpetual funnelings,
so swelling livers for *foie gras* ...

And French hens, too: the corn-fed evidence
in plucked skin's buttery-sheen,
the jaundiced haunches, yellowing leg-meat,
force-fed plumpness ...

But in Famine Ireland
force-feeding never entered Whig thinking:
for when demand for corn-meal grew,
Lord Russell ordered the closure of Poorhouse depots,
so battening the destitute down with hunger
evidenced in their swivelling distressed eyes,

starvation limbs,
visible gizzards,
the jaundice-yellow of relapsing fever,
livers swelling to collapsing,
the stink of dysentery,
the pang and pain
of passing the buck,
and passing the buck …

IV: Task Work

"The works should be unproductive so as to impose limits on the applications for employment-schemes"
        C. E. Trevelyan, Memorandum of August 1st, 1846

They gave them task work:
low hills to lower, meadows to level,
hollows to fill, rivers to dig deeper,
fallen walls to stand tall, fields to square off
and boundaries to build around acres
of grass-land walling nothing in but hares.

Gave them lines on their maps:
"meal roads" going nowhere,
tracks across mountain and bog
bringing nothing to no-one
and not meant to be travelled
so mostly unfinished, unusable if,
and built for thruppence per day with
two splats of stirabout's wetted maize
eaten off spades swiped twice on grass.

They gave them breaking of stone:
silver sweeps of hammers, the liftings
and falls with dull thuds like hollow barrels,
the slicings of light as splitting stone
into moon-halves, odd sparks glinting,
and rock splintering to chippings
for packing potholes in coach-roads:
tons done by hand, mothers and children
at penny-ha'pence a day, squatting
as knocking rock against rock.

Gave them shalings in baskets and creels,
women reeling at barrow-wheeling
till abandoning stone-piles by roadsides,
their own funeral pyres.

They gave them task work: heavy and hard.
And grimmer still as winter fingered in
under bitter winds and snow, with hungrier folk
spraunged on haunches waiting for neighbours to fall
and pellagra, marasmus, starvation
staking their claim.

They gave them stone-walling
with never a reckoning
it might cost them their lives.

Gave them stone.

V: *Summing Up*

George Charles Bingham was good with sums.

Born the year of the Act of Union, 1800
at age 26 had mastered the practice of addition
and by a series of calculations had arrived at
his formula for living: "Bingham's Dandies".
Being smart, added this to his Castlebar baronetcy.
Didn't challenge any theorems, despite going off
at a tangent – overseas in England – where became
absentee landlord, his estates leftover to land-agents,
the O'Malleys, who grappled with long divisions
of land, and the multiplications of tenant-families.

Further calculations, without showing his workings,
returned Bingham as Mayo's M.P. His method?
Polling votes from neighbour Major Fitzgerald's tenants: 1826
no proofs needed to test frequency of repeat patterns.

A decade later, retiring to his estates on army half-pay,
this pure maths genius put an acute angle on his accounts
and figuring the O'Malleys - lowest common denominators -
had excelled themselves in subtraction of rents,
reduced their function to the power of none.

To clear next decade's slate took up applied mathematics.
His simple solution to statistical problems: massive subtraction
of 2000 tenants from Ballinrobe parish, no other remainders 1847
and by unequal equation, putting nothing to nothing,
found the surplus recurring, and Castlebar Poorhouse overfull.

Yes, brilliant with figures, this George Charles Bingham;
his highest common factor, his title: Third Lord Lucan.

But then, number-crunching runs in the family:
brother-in-law, Lord Cardigan, having totted up
£30,000 (at contemporary value) for his commission as Colonel
managed in half an hour at Balaclava to reduce
without differentiation
673 men to 113 dead and 134 wounded,
then integrated the equation with the loss of 497 horses -
a result which flabbergasted the Nation;   1854

and, four generations on, the Seventh Earl,
graduating to a higher degree,   November, 1974
foxed his peers by solving the unsolvable:
how to take self away from self
and leave nothing behind ...

"George Charles Bingham…was a professional soldier… which is to say he knew and cared more about pretty uniforms than the management of men. By a series of purchases he became lieutenant-colonel commanding one of the smartest cavalry regiments in the British army, the 17th Lancers – 'Bingham's Dandies'."
    Robin Neillands, **Walking Through Ireland** (1993), page 77

The Politics of Class

I: Poor-man's racehorse

I recall Uncle Bill telling how in times past
the gentry snipped the leg-tendons and lopped
off toes so maiming these peasant-bred hounds
into ratting-dogs, no way fit for hunting deer
or stags, and handicapping them to be housed
in our back-to-back terraces, our streets.

Not like school secretary Ms. Sally Anderson's
standard poodle. (She lives along a drive.) He's
a real *Dandini* of pampering, with his arrogant
stance, his *café-au-lait* curls cropped into pom-
pommed pipe-cleaner tail, and those banded ruffs
above hock, above stifle, so really looks the part
until he collapses to a daft whirling-dervishing
as trying to lick his dick's wax-crayon.
                            No point then
putting hands together for this gundog-retriever
that's brought nothing back but slippers.

Gloria, Bill's cream-sleek whippet, is another story.
She's wind-skinny, as if eating's beneath her. See
her leash of a tongue, beseeching eyes, her soft-paw
padding, her nudging at doors. The elegant dignity
of her longish lope, her resting calm, as big of heart,
slow beating, she dozes by the fireside.
                            No kidding, she's a belter!
Watch her lolloping full stride – legs a stretched X –
as not half giving those leverets runs for his money.

Thrives on Bill's praise, and the lights of hares.

II: Class Act

The Andersons' birds, an excess of twenty,
in netted enclosure: mopsing orioles, sad parakeets,
songless canaries, zebra-finches paling away to grey.
With their stale pool, and waste of tree splattered
next to death, they remained alien, seemed asleep,
their droppings as mean as grit.

And ours: nowhere doves, but randy backyard pigeons,
all warble, flap and scattered corn. Their coral pink toes.
Jewel-box throats. Their sashaying ways.
Trained to race, were eager performers – shuffling
and shimmying, heads bobbing with a throbbing pulse.
Knew for sure there's no place like home. Graced it.

Feathered friends. Theirs; ours.
More than streets apart.

III: Classy statues

Placed in the leaded windowbay
and angled to catch the afternoon sun,
the Andersons' souvenir of Empire:
that carved peasant fisherman
with the sinuous beauty that resides in poverty -
robes scooped clear of water,
his arcing rod,
the brace of dangling carp.

How its patina-mix of beeswax
and fingering shouted arrival,
the confirmation of class.

I pictured its chiseller,
sitting cross-legged for days,
chipping and whittling
the rhythmic limb of wood,
its down of shavings
so richly chestnut
as he made the face take shape:
the almond eyes, that wily smile,
the all of it, inhabiting a world
so much farther out beyond our world:
those other lives, other ways, other gods.

Our "farther out" was Father Dykes –
always a one for a laugh. And yet,
no joke that confirmation souvenir of his:
the mass-produced plaster statuette
which Mum centred on our mantelshelf -
the hung-eyed manikin pinned to the cross:
God's own take on otherworldliness,
the fisherman of men.

The Black & White Divisions

We reckoned we were holding ground, doing
all right – if not winning – till they brought in
the horses, towering powerfully above us, profiles
sharp-lined, their blacks and browns gleaming
in sunlight, or glistening under drizzle. Not to
mention the almost sculpted under-muscle running
beneath coat; their angled flanks; head tossing
with dismissive snorts; the liquid whinnying;
the empty clacks of hooves.

It was their calmness that alarmed even
when pressed up close to us. And though most of us
had spent years away from horses and the ways
of horses, we'd been taught from kids to respect
things in authority, so had no option but to look
up to their gliding eyes, the curtainings of mane,
the arcs of neck - so different from that daily
cage-plunge, our hearts bump-thumping, into
darkness then thwacking, backs bowed, at seams
three feet thick, hacking on our knees the hard
black bands that shaled away to thungeing lumps
in the dust.

The News and telly underplayed this side of things.
Framed us rabble-rousers bringing Britain to its knees;
ridiculed our leader Fascist-loony-become-Leftist-beast;
and called him daft at that.

Now, several decades later, they want a remake-replay.
And I recall reading somewhere History repeats itself:
the first time around as tragedy; the second as comedy.

Some joke! They forget how we'd roared. And cried.

Our voices lost in the black and white divisions of class,
that September '84; our Histories revised.

Moving On:
Jo, the Crossing Sweeper from *Bleak House*

His is the certainty of mud, wheels, whips, horses;
his familiars, the swish of bristles, dresses, petticoats, the click of heels;
his purlieu, the extended palm.

Escorting his broomwalk between ziggurats of horse-dung
and civilization's detritus, this vagabond highwayman
inhabits the lowest rank in the taxonomy of crossing sweepers:

> the professional
> the occasional
> the Lucus-a-non
> the crippled
> the morning
> the Sunday
> the maimed
> the deformed
> the juvenile.

Common creature of the common streets,
>   homely filth begrimes him
>   homely parasites devour him
>   homely sores are in him
>   homely rags are on him,
he is Dickens' genuine made-at-home article with no home.

"Dedlocked" out of society to subsist on its fringes;
"Tulkinghorned" for information, then shoved onto the streets,
he perpetuates the illnesses visited upon him by spreading them
at gentry's expense – ask Esther, face to face –
and relays poverty's grasping baton to drifts of city-spillage:
>   the squeegee traffic-lads in Jo'burg, New York, Darwin,
>   the street-gleaners of Dublin, Delhi, Cairo, Aswan,

Shares with them the mantra of departure

Move on   Move on   Move on   Move on

Testament, for sure, that the poor are always with us.

Fishing the Khabur River, Syria

This was once our sacred river,
so sacred that we were forbidden
even to drink from it.

Yet today we fish in it.
See Youssef there, waist-deep,
straddling mid-stream, braced against
the current under the arching bridge
where the river swirls quicker, darker
in curdled eddies that chunter the pebbles
shuttling forward and catch whatever
rattles snagging downstream.

See how his back tenses, his muscles
defined beneath his splashed didashah,
his checked ghutra trailing flaglike over
his shoulder, one arm reaching out, the other
anchored with twined sisal to the bank-side,
and he's stretching and straining, his fingers
seeking beneath the chilled depths in a leaning feel,
the water suddenly muddied as if by blood.

And he has one. A heaving haul, struggling
to make it secure, dragging in - heavy, slow -
fumbling its slipping dip, and passing it back
to the bank-side down our line of men where
they lift it, up and over, then across, one after
the other, wet forms glistening silvery
till placed with dignity face down.

Four times today we have done this -
Omar, Khalid, Sayeed, Ahmed -
and now the boy Mohammed.

But for Rasha and Almira, our mothers,
it is too much. They bow their heads, turn
backs, and melt away home,
their abayas closing in on them
like closed doors as they go.

Surely Allah has forsaken us.

See these five,
hands tied behind backs
where the bullets found their zero.

This is the village

meting out silences between
the distilling heat of siesta
and the streets' abandonment,

the plaster-scabbed houses
leaning against each other
like a stack of cards

their blue-grey shutters
latched fast against mid-day,
the *À VENDRE* signs clear

giveaways, like the hollyhocks
teetering above pavements,
the fruit trees beyond picking,

the dahlias heading toward seed.
And there, the arched barn doors,
their unvarnished wood

flaking to woodwormed grain,
and sharing backyards with hens
scratting among geraniums,

their scarlet scars remainders
like the moss-riddled names
on the Memorial for the Great War.

And, as if on cue, a young faun,
amber-caramel, and stock-still
in surprise, mid-street

at seeing us, his shared stare
collapsing into panic
as skittering to safety away.

Salles Lavalette, Poitou-Charentes

Gran's Living-Room Triptych

I   Married at nineteen, Gran had given birth to her
family of five: all sons – one stillborn, one dead
in infancy, the remaining three buttonholed by
Granddad into a manly household, though Gran

thought she controlled it all by silences and looks,
hence her pick of *Whistler's Mother* in greys and
black with its grim calm, the still hands crossed
on her lap in a monumental solidness islanded

by silence, her seated profile demurely dressed
in a sort of Puritan assurance of just what Gran
aspired to: that grace of motherhood without trace
of having suffered the trials of a broken household.

II   She'd balanced this with *The Laughing Cavalier*
with his attractive fanciness, that self-satisfied
arrogance of smile, his eye-lights almost louche,
the flouncing, lacy tracery and dandified brocade,

his rakish hat and feather-flourish, daft enough
to make you want to break your face to laughter.
Besides, he had on his lips the same ambiguous mix
of distance and arrival that helped fix Granddad as

church-verger, with always that smile underwriting
his eyes as if more was going-on than he dared to share,
like the lip-shushing finger when his sons stumbled on
the beers he'd concealed beneath heaped chicken-feeds.

III No coincidence that keeping these apart, she chose
that childhood trial: the divide between telling lies and
betrayal in *And When Did You Last See Your Father?*
with its ransacked linen chest and snaffled trinket box,

the huddled wife and mother, her sniffling daughter
gently held by Cromwellian halberdier, and her son
islanded in profiled defiance, his sky-blue satin suit
with chased lace collar and flouncings of brocade,

his face a stilled innocence and hands held crossed
behind his back as out-staring the menacing threats
that dressed the questioner's lips with those looks
and silences which Gran half-smilingly admired.

Saving face with Grandpa
and not being huffed

I catch him hovering at our lounge doorway,
face beaming though something behind his eyes
suggests he's not certain where he is, or whether
he should be here, his mind silent-film-flicking

for names, his lips teasing words around shapes
in a hesitancy belying ninety years of his tackling
things head on and giving no ground to getting old:
till, *Draughts, Grandpa? You're black* – and he

makes straight for the board's chequered territory
of dare. Once settled in his usual chair, he's all
kept breath and concentrated energy while he
puts his strategies to work: that ruse of losing

one piece to jump my two; or the leap-frogging
zigzag across the squares as he deftly pincer-picks
my yellow-white discs. And I can't help thinking
his men know every winning move, their kingings

assured in his surety of game-play. He's good,
and knows it, though I grudgingly convince myself
some of his skill is the stuff of years - after all,
he is last century … Then comes the final steal:

his triumphant run, jack-jumping with a clacking
accuracy that removes two, three, four black kings.
He laughs his little laugh, *Like life! It's just a game.
Best in both worlds, you know, not being huffed!*

I squirm – not at his jibe, but in pretence of another
loss. (Recall, this time around I'm white, he's black.)
And wonder whether it's guile, forgetfulness, or age
that defines the ritual behind his saving face ...

In draughts, when a player does not take an opponent's piece (either deliberately or by failing to see it), the piece that could have made the jump is *huffed*, i.e. removed.
"To be huffed" is the adoption of a resentful or piqued mood usually as a result of someone else's behaviour.

Soldiering

i.m. Granddad Charles

I   Think shell cases. Their brass
not hammered, chased, and trimmed
between pounding rounds to trench-art vase
or ornamental tin for cigarette-spill.
But as they were. Streamlined, clean,
glistening under the sheen of sun.

No wonder he souvenired them home,
secreted deep within his army uniform.
Silent reminders. Upright. Disposable.
Spent. Like him.

II   Recall him, dirty? Not ever.
His workday clothes always pressed
with his medal of half-hunter pinned
at his chest. His shoes spat-and-bulled
till beaming like his cheeks. And hair
Brylcreem-sleeked. Never mussed.

Can't picture him floundering in the piled
high trench for hours, or up to the shin
in sliding mire, his hair alive with lice,
and senses frazzled by those crashing skies ...
the thuds ... the stench ... the din ...

III   Watched him take a chicken
and wring its neck in hands-on flicks
as instinctive as blinking.

Seen him ridding the vermin-run,
lobbing the dead rat at the crackling fire
and counting down its grim explosion.

Noticed him, finger on trigger,
aiming to miss as scaring the fox
from Gran's hen-pen. But nothing bigger.

Cannot imagine him ever shouldering a gun
to kill a man. Then again, he never let on
how the army did for him. Just kept mum,

and soldiered on.

North Ferriby Foreshore, remembering
i.m. Granddad Charles and Peter Reading who never met

Not sand, but reaches of mudflat
veined by rainbowy seawater-seeps
along the Humberside strand. And,
further out, a pewter gleam where
the Trent – water within water –
fattens to estuary's broad blade, then
wider still, circle-swirls to mouth
at silent horizons, the North Sea,
Europe and beyond.

Seems worlds away from Trent's
well-head and its insignificant sibilants
trickling through Bailey's farmyard.

How memories tumble. To hills.
And home: the moorland village
cricked safe in England's vertebrae
where gritstone walling collects
the fields' purposes.

And to Granddad – simple man
crowned local bigwig – mouthing down
his home-grown workmates,
Thait senatucked.*

Laugh at that. That bastardised Latin
he hadn't even had chance to learn
let alone forget, any more than he'd
heard of Ferriby. Or estuary.
Though knew belonging,
like the sons of his name.

---

* North Staffordshire dialect for "You're sinew-tight; i.e. worn-out, exhausted."

Peter Reading's poem, *Dog's Tomb*, (**Untitled**, 2001) contains the lines,

"QVI CAECVS ET SENECTVTE CONFECTVS.
  Who blindness and senility prepared"

Being Waspish

… our neighbour said right from the start,
No good will come of it.
By *"it"* she meant billeting the Yanks
in Stannard's shirt-mill, where they bunked up
between the greasy reek of stilled machines
and the cotton-bales piled high.

That was the third year of the war,
that year our railings went for the war-effort
and like her son never came back.
The time of black-outs, with gas-lamps unlit
and the nightly Luftwaffe raids
droning overhead to Manchester and Liverpool,
one plane crash-landing on the Moor,
wing-bits and photographs of Billy Brown
with trophied goggles on show in the bobby's-shop.

It was that time, too, of weekly ARP dances,
and, for sure, those GIs were having the time
of their lives judging how the Methodists –
Primitives and Wesleyans – united in their chinwagging
as the Yanks be-bopped, jitterbugged and smooched
the night away with the mill-girls,
then traded favours for fags, gum and stockings;
our neighbour japing, *Don't get owt for nowt.*

And was right again.

Evidence: that clutch of GI kids
filling prams the next Spring,
their Afro-Carib faces so out-of-place -
the real sting in the tail –
in our waspy town.

The Longest Day

Not the heroics of John Wayne
spearing across D-Day beaches
while extras get blown to bits.

Not fish-face Robert Mitchum
leaping into the sea and wading ashore,
his rifle carried high to keep it dry.

Not Richard Todd, steel-eyed
and stiff-upper-lipped, revisiting
Pegasus Bridge.

Not even Kenneth More trying to hide
behind a beard as Beach-Master Colin Maud
roaring "Get off this blasted shore".

But hundreds of fameless men being strafed
in that vastness of sand and cloud
with nothing to hide behind but fear,

two planes raining bullets and noise –
wave after harrying wave –
the menacing, the menaced.

Watching that, you remember
standing stranded, exposed
in slow-motion monochrome

hour after hour and so alone
by your Dad's hospital bed

your moment's longest day.

Of the spaces between

Ays senatucked they reckon, these blokes
supping in the pub, their callused palms
flatly miming out their sad prognosis.
Senatucked, n borsant. Wunna towk. *

Not Punjabi, you bet. Not Urdu either. But
could be just as foreign, given the puzzled
frowns newcomers make, their minds tracking
across deserts, vast plains, anyplace but here.

Yet I know these words. Have grown up
with their talk alongside my 'proper' tongue -
that ritual of schoolkid English which taught
me to keep the spaces between our worlds.

And know, too, he's not always been
like this, my Dad. Has worked gang-side
with them, sharing their laughs and banter,
sweat tracking down backs and forearms,

their brows burnished in the furnace glow
of the rolling mill, its clanging anvils,
leaps of flame, and shushing steam.
That's till the lay-offs. Then he faded

wordlessly away. Stayed sitting for hours
at home, eyes deadly drilling into hands,
with silences so deep even the gangman's
Staffordshire twang couldn't shift him and

he became what he is today, a refugee
of dialect. *Senatucked.* And talkless.
Though doesn't need words to show
he's aware I understand that it's more

than space between us we've refined.

---

*North Staffordshire dialect: "He's worn out ...Worn out and bored. Won't talk."

senatucked cf the Latin *senectu*s elderly, old-aged; and the Spanish *senectud*, becoming old.

Patchwork Language:

for Ruth, Sarah, Ro

You've amassed this stash of material -
scraps, samples, hand-me-downs -
colourful stuff you just have to possess,
make your own, hoard for future use;
though, never knowing their wealth's extent,
are reduced to trusting their potential as they
push themselves to be re-used.

Their first trick's the best: letting you
think you're in control as you arrange what
you've imagined as fit for purpose -
say, a range of shades in subtleties of tone,
balancing dark against light, and suited to
the backing and padding underpinning the scheme,
for, after all, what lies behind and in-between
adds meanings to the surface reading.

Next, they offer you the option of following
a traditional pattern, drafting it out on paper,
framing block after block, but taking care
your material's not skewed and stretched
against the grain;
                        or, since you class yourself
master of your craft, you're allowed to interpret it
at will, filling in the shape, picking out the rhythm,
and stitching-through the visual imagery
in keeping with your theme.

                    Either way,
they know you'll need to allocate yourself
some latitude to accommodate all the skill,
imagination and time that's been invested –

for that, a wiggly line can be most forgiving –

                         though, take note:
too much attention spent plotting metres into feet,
or using material that's skimpy –

        filigree and gossamer scrunch puckering up –

might just frustrate your grand designs,

even blow a poem's cover.

Shoplifting

Thinking about it, it's only practical
to cover your tracks. Like picking things up
mid-take, and putting them back again,
trying them for size, for fit - *does it suit?* -
setting them against what you've already got
et cetera, et cetera ... Then, I suppose,
the trick's acting naturally, as if
it doesn't matter being seen in possession.

While you might find it difficult
to begin with, you'll get spoilt
for choice in time, till you end up
spending ages wondering which line
to select, or if it's worth it after all.

And, yes, you could smuggle
the coloureds in – say, heliotrope, magenta -
but then there isn't any need to attract
excess attention. No, go carefully,
stealthily even, between the stacks
of what's on offer. Style counts.

And covering those absences -
what's right, what works, what to leave -
needs loads of practice, though if it's
drafted craftily it will pay handsomely.
(That's travelling hopefully of course.)

But then, occasionally, the goods
are too good to pass unnoticed. So
once that buzzer goes and you become
the centre of folks' attention,
it's best owning up to being in possession.
After all, at this stage of things,
there's no use being stumped for words.

Could even be worth taking credit for.

"A poem is … a prime bit of shoplifting where you get something out the door before the buzzer goes off."
Nuala Ni Dhomhnaill, July 1995

Roger Elkin has won 60 First Prizes in (inter)national Poetry Competitions and several awards, including the *Sylvia Plath Award for Poems about Women* (1986*)*, and the *Howard Sergeant Memorial Award for Services to Poetry* (1987). **Sheer Poetry** is his twelfth collection; his previous collections include ***Fixing Things*** (2011); ***Bird in the Hand*** (2012); ***Marking Time*** (2013); and ***Chance Meetings*** (2014). Editor of *Envoi,* (1991 – 2006), he is available for readings, workshops and poetry competition adjudication.